Béla
BARTÓK

OLD HUNGARIAN DANCES

from *Hungarian Peasant Songs, Sz.71*

Orchestrated by

Clark McAlister

Study Score
Partitur

SERENISSIMA MUSIC, INC.

ORCHESTRA

2 Flutes (2nd also Piccolo)

2 Oboes

2 Clarinets (B-flat, A)

2 Bassoons

2 Horns (F)

2 Trumpets (C)

Timpani

Triangle

Violin I

Violin II

Viola

Violoncello

Double Bass

Duration: ca.6 minutes

Composed 1914-18 for piano.
The present selction is a new orchestration of Nos.7-15
of the 15 Hungarian Peasant Songs, Sz.71
first published in 1920 by Universal Edition, Vienna.

ISMN: 979-0-58042-608-6

Engraved by Giuliano Forghieri

OLD HUNGARIAN DANCES

I

BÉLA BARTÓK
Orchestrated by Clark McAlister

42875

2

22
28
1
Fl.
2
take Picc.
Ob.
Cl.
Bsn.
Hn.
1
Vn.
2
Va.
Vc.
D.B.
pesante
pesante
30
sim.

4

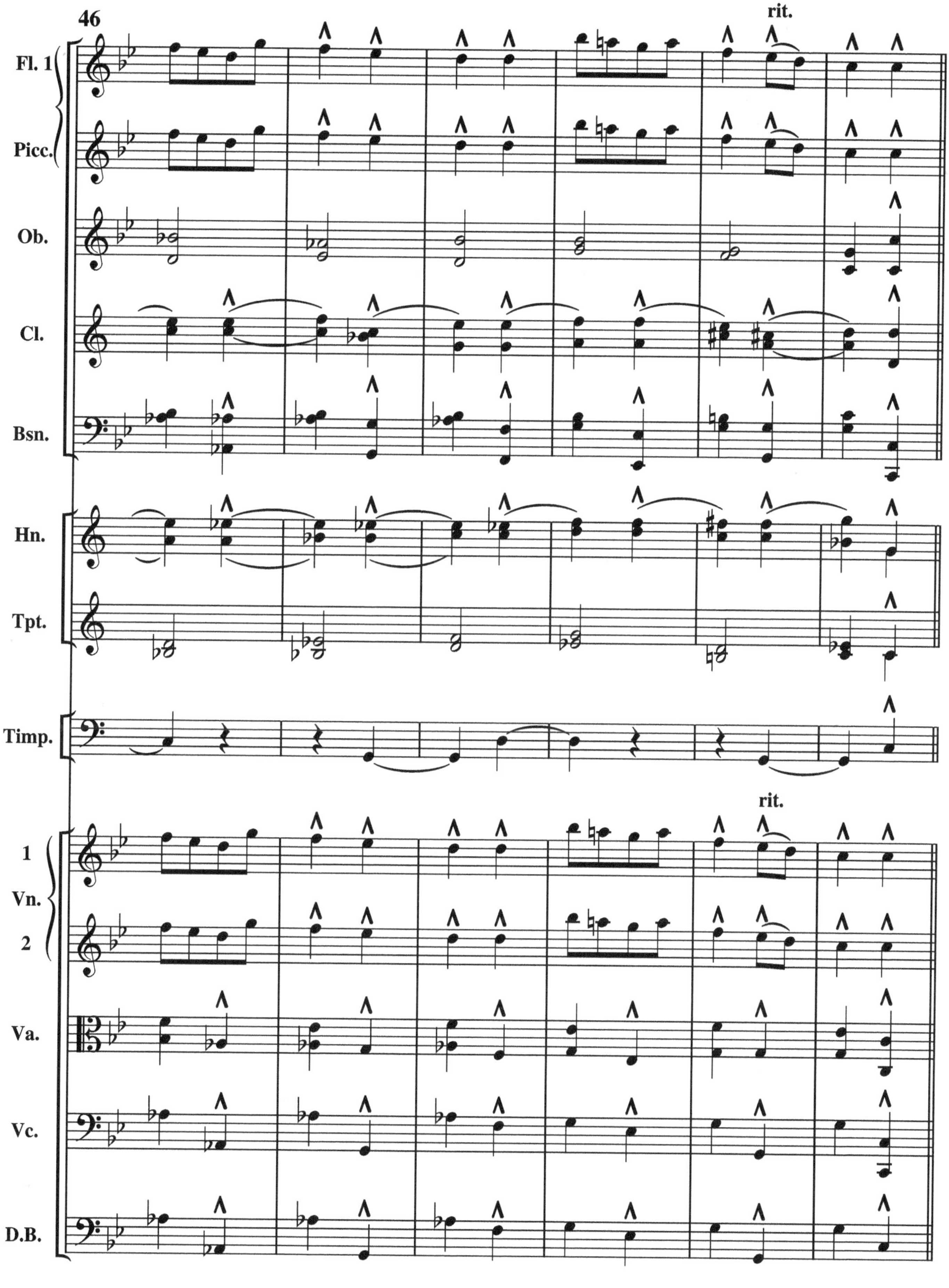
46
rit.
Fl. 1
Picc.
Ob.
Cl.
Bsn.
Hn.
Tpt.
Timp.
rit.
1
Vn.
2
Va.
Vc.
D.B.

6

II

64
tranquillo
solo
p dolce
Fl. 1
1
Vn.
2
p
p
Va.
p
Vc.
p
D.B.
70
risoluto
Fl. 1
mf
1.
Ob.
p
mf
risoluto
1
Vn.
2
mf
mf
Va.
mf
Vc.
mf
D.B.

III

Allegretto ♩= 138
76
1.
Ob.
f pesante
Tpt.
1. str. mute
f pesante
mute out
Allegretto ♩= 138
1
Vn.
2
f pesante
Va.
f
Vc.
f
D.B.
f
84
Fl. 1
f pesante
Picc.
Picc.
f pesante
Ob.
a 2
f pesante
Cl.
a 2
f pesante
Bsn.
f
Hn.
sf
sf
sf
Tpt.
1. (open)
f
2. f
1
Vn.
2
f pesante
Va.
Vc.
div.
D.B.

92
L'istesso tempo
solo
Picc.
p leggero
Cl.
1. solo
p leggero
92
L'istesso tempo
1
Vn.
2
p leggero
p leggero
Va.
p leggero
Vc.
unis.
p leggero
D.B.
100
Picc.
p
Cl.
1.
p
Hn.
1.
p
2.
p
pizz.
pizz.
pizz.

108
Fl. 1
Picc.
Ob.
a 2
Cl.
a 2
Bsn.
Hn.
Tpt.
1.
2.
Timp.
108
arco
1
Vn.
2
arco
arco
Va.
Vc.
D.B.

116
Fl. 1
Picc.
Ob.
Cl.
Bsn.
Hn.
Tpt.
Timp.
Vn.
Va.
Vc.
D.B.
più f
a 2
1.
2. più f
div.
unis.
f

IV

124
Assai moderato ♩= 100-104
(rhythm of three measures)
Ob.
Cl.
Bsn.
Hn.
Tpt.
Timp.
f
1. Ob. 2
Assai moderato ♩= 100-104
(rhythm of three measures)
div.
f pesante (ma sostenuto)
sim.
Vn. 1
Vn. 2
Va.
Vc.
D.B.
Bsn. 2, one player
136
a 2
f pesante (ma sostenuto)
sim.
unis.
div.
(tutti)

148
1
Fl.
2
f
f
Ob.
più f
a 2
Cl.
più f
Bsn.
più f
Hn.
a 2
più f
Tpt.
più f
Timp.
f
148
1
Vn.
2
più f
div.
più f
Va.
più f
unis.
Vc.
più f
pesante
(ma sostenuto)
D.B.
più f

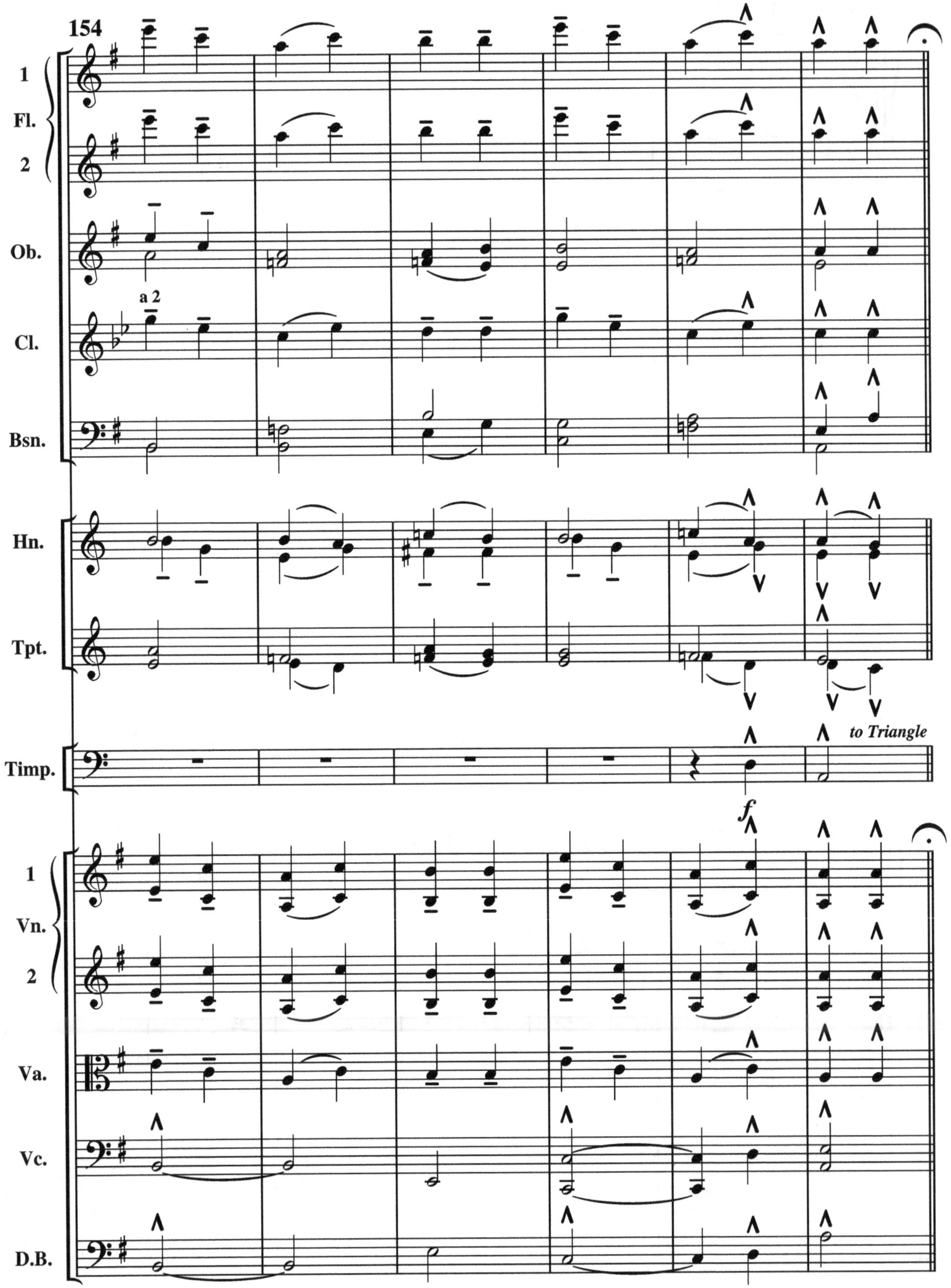
154
Fl.
1
2
Ob.
a 2
Cl.
Bsn.
Hn.
Tpt.
to Triangle
Timp.
f
Vn.
1
2
Va.
Vc.
D.B.

V

160
Allegretto ♩ = 112
Fl. 1 2
p leggero
sf
Cl.
Bsn.
Hn.
1.
p
Trgl.
Triangle
Vn. 1 2
pizz.
Va.
Vc.
D.B.
165
Ob.
2.
solo
arco
tutti
pizz.

170
Fl. 1
Cl.
Bsn.
1.
p
Hn.
1.
p
170
1
Vn.
2
Va.
Vc.
D.B.
175
calando
G.P.
Fl. 1
più p
pp
Cl.
più p
pp
calando
G.P.
1
Vn.
2
Va.
solo
arco
Vc.
più p
D.B.

181
Poco più vivo ♩= 138
Ob.
Bsn.
Hn.
1.
2. Bsn. 2
181
Poco più vivo ♩= 138
1
Vn.
2
Va.
Bsn. 2, one player
(arco)
one player
pizz.
Vc.
one player
pizz.
D.B.
189
1
Fl.
2
Ob.
2.
1.
Cl.
Bsn.
Hn.
Ob. 2, one player (arco)
1
Vn.
2
Va.
Vc.
D.B.

18

42875

VI

221
223
Fl.
Ob.
Cl.
Bsn.
Hn.
Tpt.
Vn.
Va.
Vc.
D.B.
a 2
2. Ob. 2
muted
div.
unis.
Bsn. 2
one player
(tutti)
229
p poco marc.
(muted)

237
poco rit.
Fl. 1 2
Ob.
Cl.
Bsn.
Hn.
Tpt.
Vn. 1 2
Va.
Vc.
D.B.
div.
unis.
VII
246
Allegro ♩ = 138
1. muted
Timpani, soft sticks
Timp.
pizz.
mf sf
pp

254
1. solo
Ob.
Hn.
Tpt.
Timp.
1
Vn.
2
Va.
Vc.
D.B.
f
sf
262
2. f
1. Ob. 2
Cl.
muted
2. f

270
Fl. 1 2
f
Ob.
più f
Cl.
più f
Bsn.
f
Hn.
f
Tpt.
(a 2)
Timp.
270
Vn. 1 2
Va.
f
Vc.
f
arco
D.B.
f

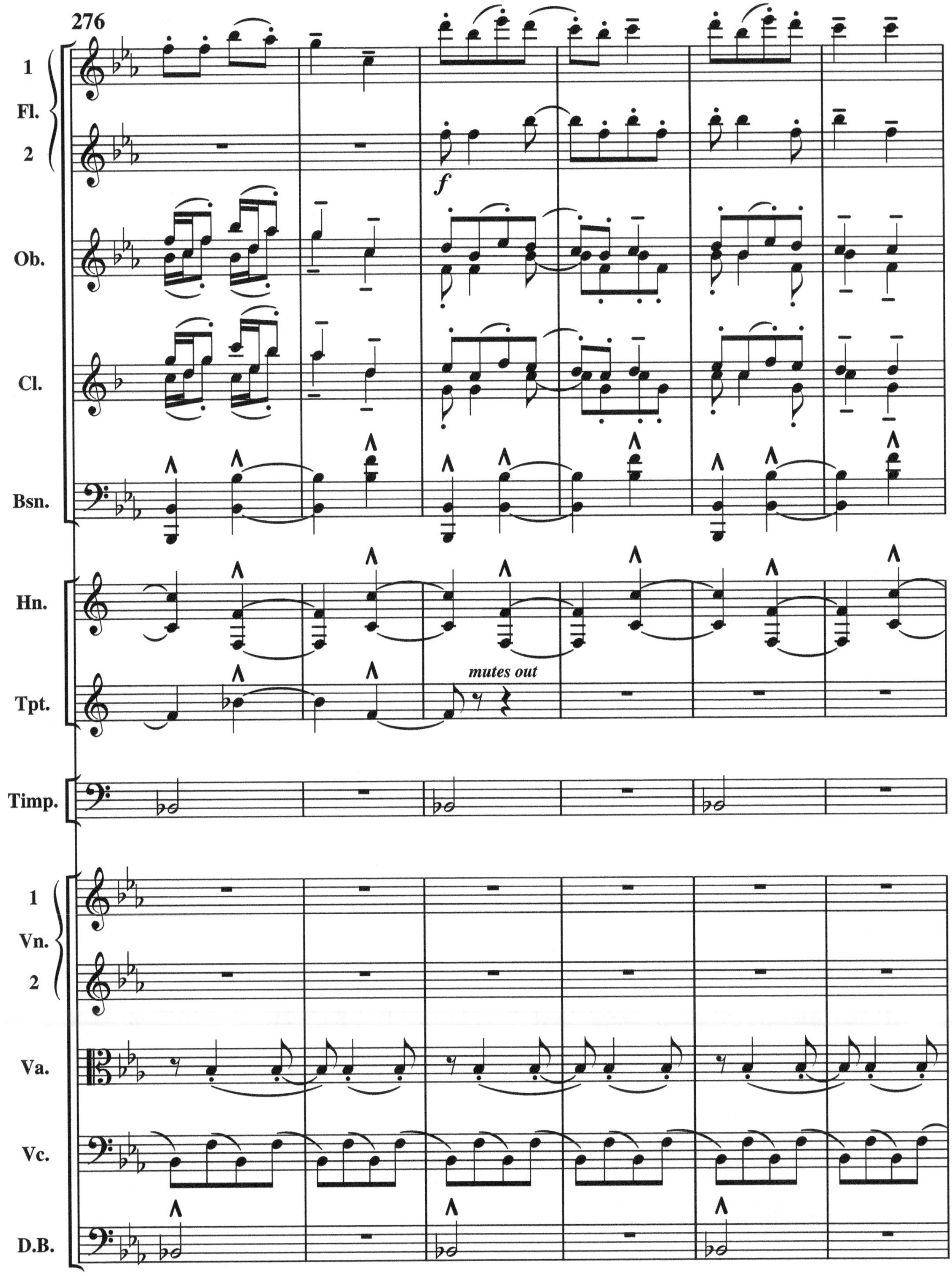
276
1
Fl.
2
Ob.
Cl.
Bsn.
Hn.
Tpt.
mutes out
Timp.
1
Vn.
2
Va.
Vc.
D.B.
f

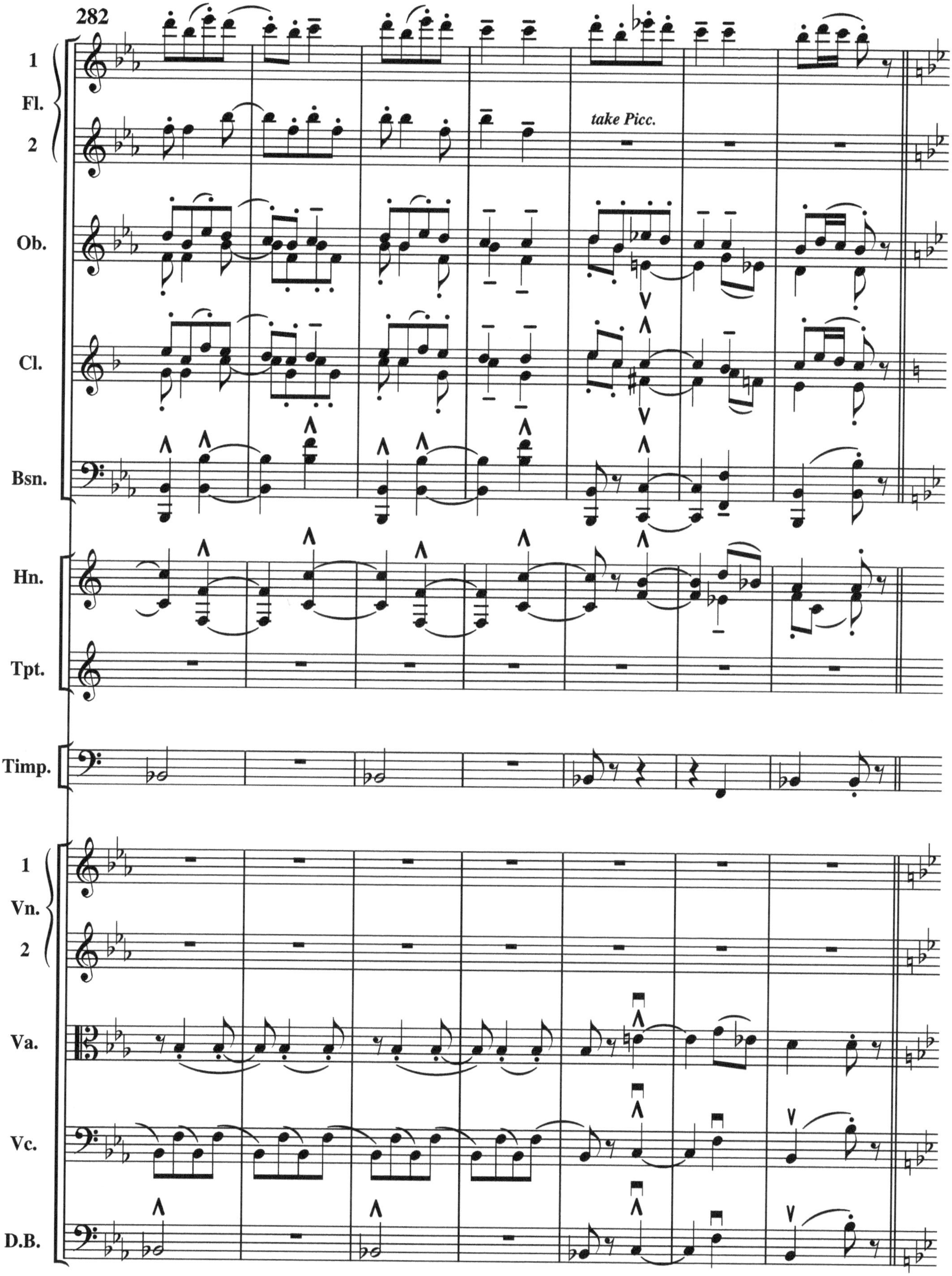
282
1
Fl.
2
take Picc.
Ob.
Cl.
Bsn.
Hn.
Tpt.
Timp.
1
Vn.
2
Va.
Vc.
D.B.

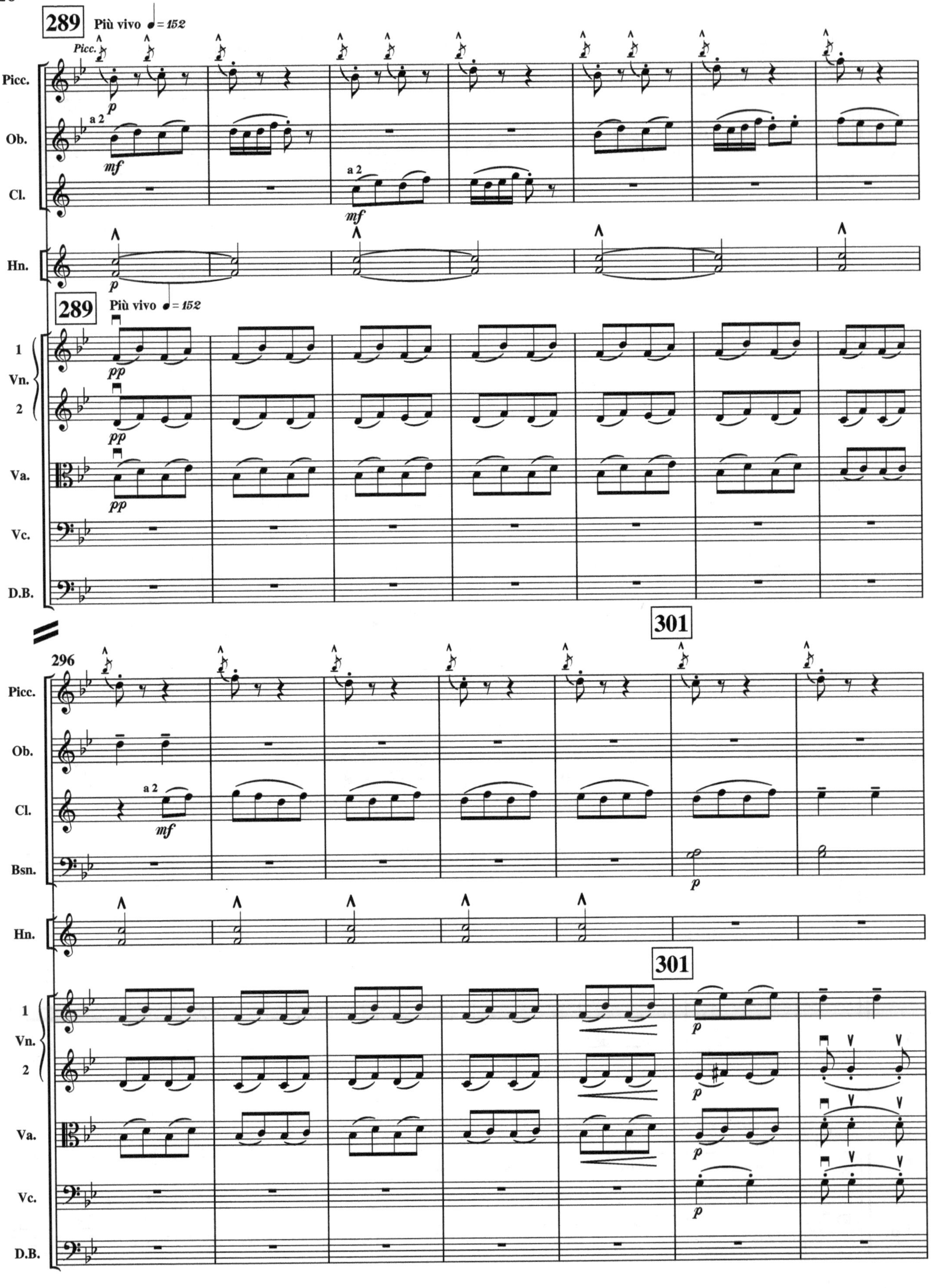

289
Più vivo ♩ = 152
Picc.
Picc.
Ob.
Cl.
Hn.
a 2
Vn.
Va.
Vc.
D.B.
296
301
Bsn.

303
Fl. 1
Picc.
Ob.
Cl.
Bsn.
Hn.
1
Vn.
2
Va.
Vc.
D.B.
mf cresc.
cresc.
a 2
mf
p cresc.
mf
sim.
310
take Flute
Tpt.
2.
f

Meno vivo ♩ = 138
318
Fl. 1
Ob.
Cl.
a 2
Hn.
Tpt.
318
Meno vivo ♩ = 138
1
Vn.
2
Oboes (div.)
Va.
Vc.
D.B.
324
1
Fl.
2
Flute
Ob.
Cl.
Bsn.
a 2
Hn.
Tpt.
1
Vn.
2
(unis.)
Va.
Vc.
D.B.

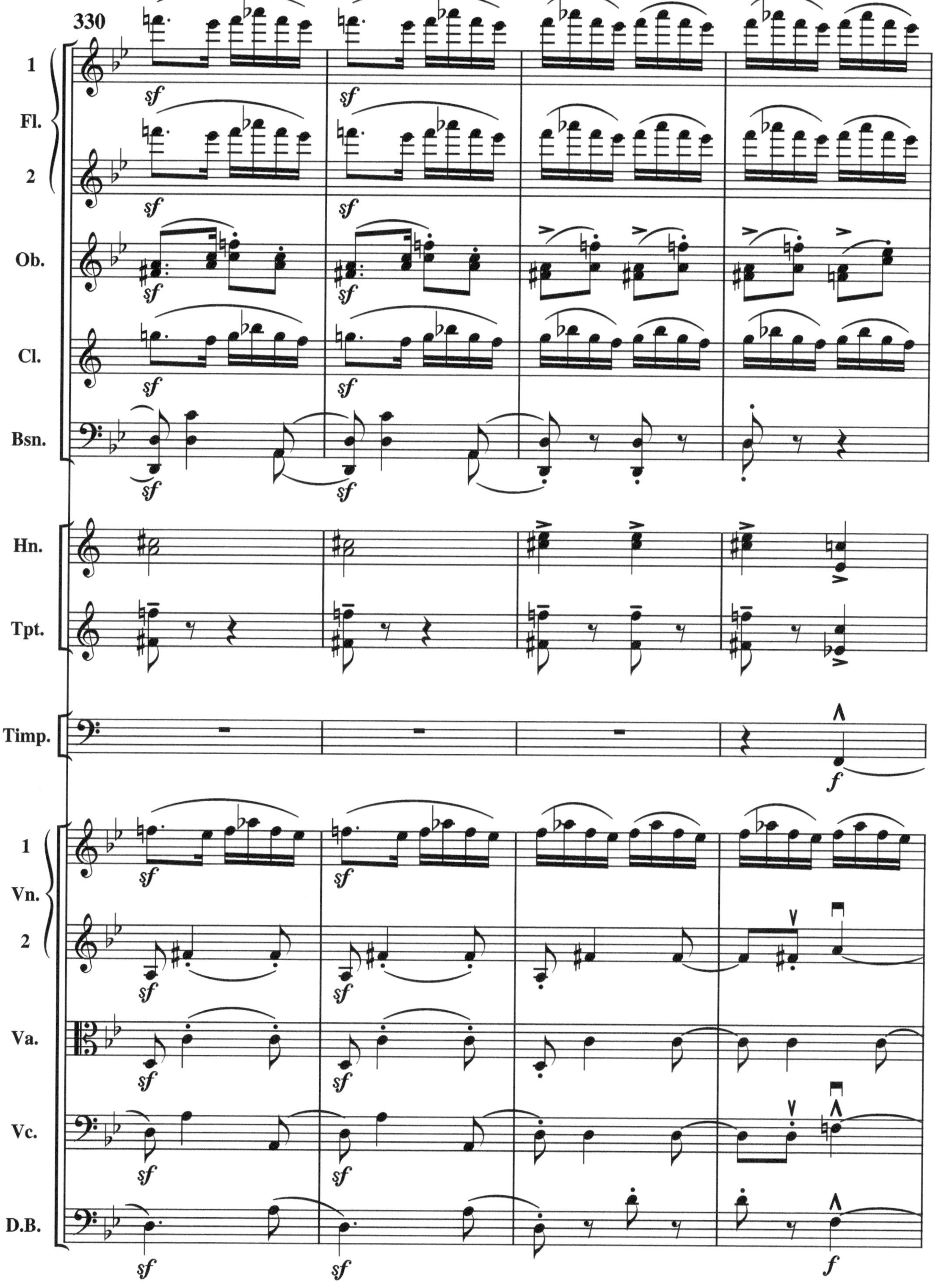
330
1
Fl.
2
Ob.
Cl.
Bsn.
Hn.
Tpt.
Timp.
1
Vn.
2
Va.
Vc.
D.B.
sf
f

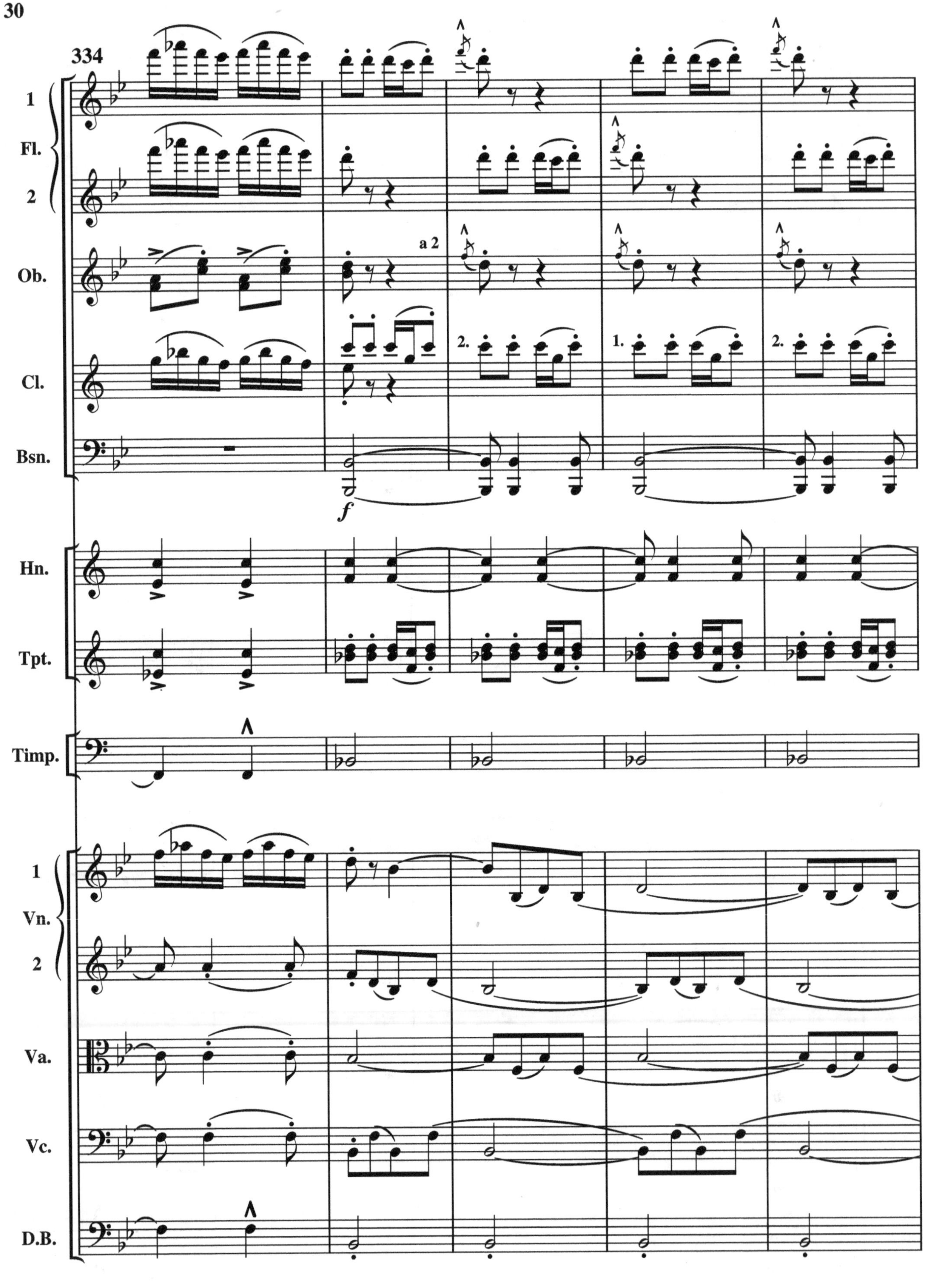
334
Fl.
1
2
Ob.
a 2
Cl.
2.
1.
2.
Bsn.
f
Hn.
Tpt.
Timp.
Vn.
1
2
Va.
Vc.
D.B.

339
1
Fl.
2
Ob.
Cl.
Bsn.
Hn.
Tpt.
Timp.
1
Vn.
2
Va.
Vc.
D.B.
dim. poco a poco
1.
f dim. poco a poco
p

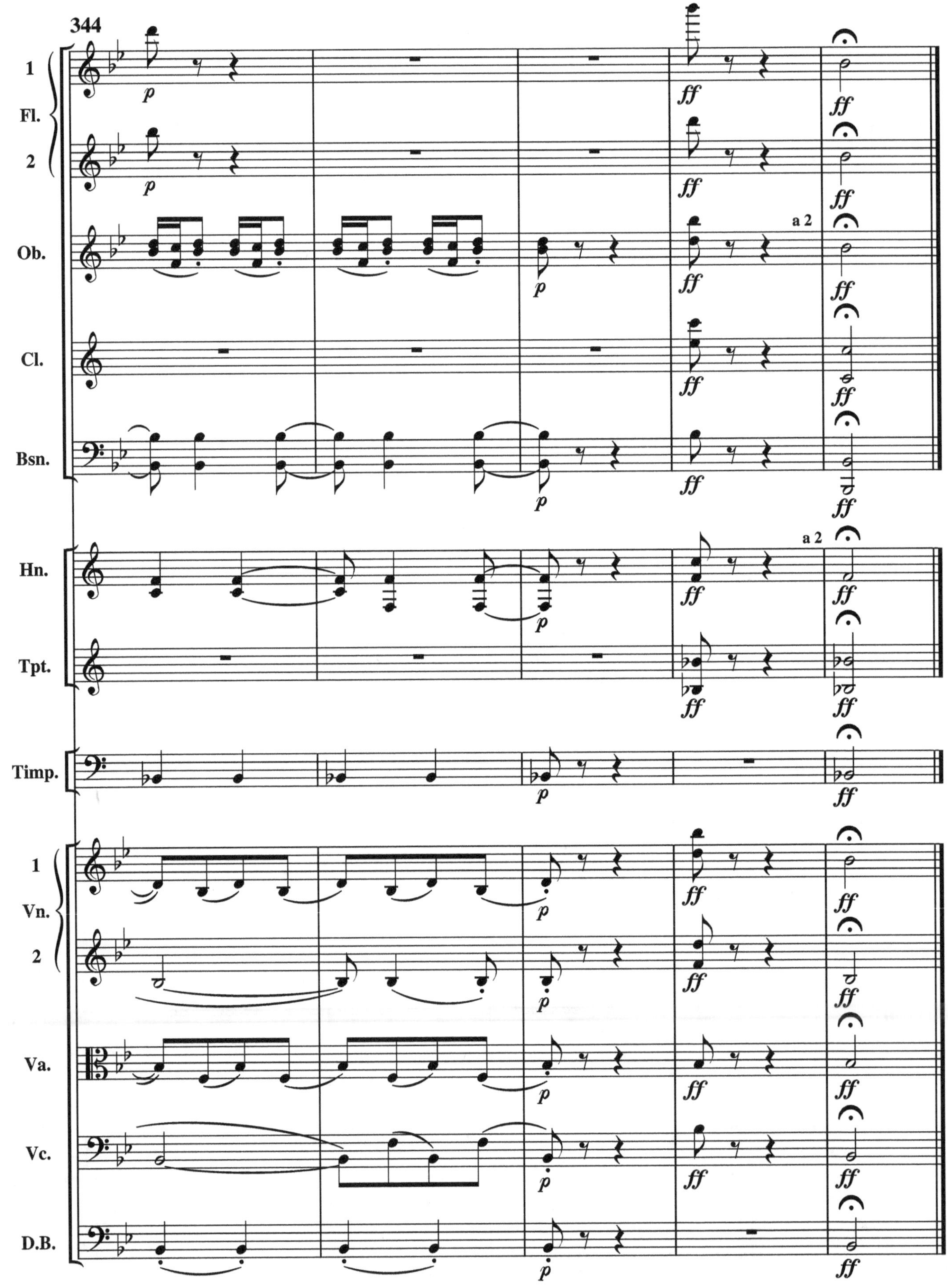
344
Fl.
1
2
Ob.
a 2
Cl.
Bsn.
Hn.
a 2
Tpt.
Timp.
Vn.
1
2
Va.
Vc.
D.B.
p
ff